· TESCO · COOKERY · COLLECTION ·

MEAT AND POULTRY

TESCO

Published exclusively for Tesco Stores Ltd.
Delamare Road, Cheshunt, Herts, EN8 9SL
by Cathay Books, 59 Grosvenor Street, London W1

First published 1985
Reprinted 1985

ISBN 0 86178 308 5

Printed in Hong Kong

ACKNOWLEDGEMENTS

The publishers would like to thank the following companies
for their kindness in providing materials and equipment
used in the photography for this book.

David Mellor, 4 Sloane Square, London SW1
Divertimenti, 139 Fulham Road, London SW3
Elizabeth David, 46 Bourne Street, London SW1
The French Kitchen and Tableware Supply Company, 86 Westbourne Grove, London W2
Graham and Green, 4 & 7 Elgin Crescent, London W11

We would also like to thank the following who were concerned in the preparation of the book.

Series Art Director Pedro Prá-Lopez
Editor Nicole Foster
Photographer Martin Brigdale (James Jackson page 30)
Stylist Sue Leighton
Food prepared for photography by Stella Murphy; Margot Mason (pages 8-9, 40, 47, 52-3)

CONTENTS

NOTE

Standard spoon measurements are used in all recipes

1 tablespoon (tbls) = one 15 ml spoon
1 teaspoon (tsp) = one 5 ml spoon
All spoon measures are level

All eggs are sizes 3 or 4 (standard) unless otherwise stated.

For all recipes, quantities are given in both metric and imperial measures.
Follow either set but not a mixture of both, as they are not interchangeable.

We set up our Consumer Advisory Service in response to the many pleas for information and cooking ideas we received from our customers. It is run by our team of qualified home economists who answer queries, offer practical advice on cookery and the home and give talks and demonstrations on new products and equipment.

The resounding success of the service and the continued demand for more and more recipes and information has now prompted us to produce our own special range of Tesco Cookery Books.

Our series starts with 12 books, each one focusing on an area that our customers have shown particular interest in. Each book contains practical background information on the chosen subject and concentrates on a wide selection of carefully tested recipes, each one illustrated in colour.

Meat and Poultry guides you through the principles of choosing, preparing and cooking a whole range of meat cuts and shows you, with step-by-step photographs, how to carve two popular joints.

The recipe collection offers an imaginative choice of dishes from simple casseroles that you can prepare in advance and freeze, to quick meat meals for a midweek supper. There is a special section on classic dishes from around the world, all beautifully illustrated and simply described. Whichever recipe you choose to try the results will be delicious, so go ahead and enjoy them all!

I very much hope you will enjoy looking through the pages which follow, trying out the recipes and above all tasting and enjoying the results. Happy Cooking!

Carey Dennis

Carey Dennis, senior home economist, Tesco Stores Ltd.

INTRODUCTION

For most of us, meat is still the main ingredient of our daily meals – and a vital source of protein, iron and vitamins. But as prices rise and less time is spent in the kitchen, it becomes increasingly necessary to get good value for money by choosing suitable recipes for the meat we buy.

The recipes in this book are grouped under different headings, depending on the type of meal you want to cook.

Casseroles are the perfect standby for all types of meal, and although long slow cooking is necessary the preparation is often extremely quick, so that you can be doing other things while the casserole looks after itself.

Roasts are the traditional centrepieces of any great British meal, requiring good quality meat, careful cooking and all the familiar accompaniments.

Mince meals are the mainstay of family suppers. The selection of recipes shows that mince lends itself to an incredible variety of dishes for, of course, mince doesn't just mean minced beef!

Quick meat dishes give a real choice of things to cook when time is short. Some of the recipes are suitable for family meals while others are appropriate for entertaining.

Finally, each country has developed its own traditions in meat cookery, and has created dishes that have become famous. The variety of dishes in the *classic meat dishes* section reflects the versatility of meat, and includes simple, homely recipes as well as party specialities.

Choosing meat: The cut of meat you choose will depend on the cooking method, but there are a few general pointers to quality. In beef, the lean should be 'marbled' with small flecks of fat for moistness and flavour. The meat should feel firm but moist to the touch. It is not true to say that if beef is not bright red then it is not fresh. It is bright red when first cut but even if it is packaged immediately it will darken gradually because it is in contact with air. Better cuts of beef will be fine grained; those with a coarser texture are cheaper cuts which usually require long, slow cooking to tenderize.
In **lamb**, the meat should be fine grained and a fresh-looking pink colour. The fat should be creamy dry white.
In **pork**, the flesh should be fine grained and light pink in colour with white creamy fat. The rind should be thin and elastic.
Veal cuts are similar to beef but are paler and more tender since they come from younger animals.

Storing meat: Put meat in the refrigerator (or in a meat safe in a very cool larder) as soon as possible after purchase. Remove wrappings, place on a plate and cover loosely with cling film. Most cuts of meat will keep for 2-3 days, but cook unpackaged mince, sausages and offal the day you buy them.

The general guideline for storage of frozen raw meat is that the leaner it is the longer it will keep. In general, store offal for up to 3 months, pork up to 6 months, veal and lamb up to 9 months, beef and chicken up to 12 months.

It is possible to cook the smaller cuts of meats such as chops, steaks, cubed meat and sausages straight from the freezer provided they are started on a low heat and allowed to cook through completely. Larger joints are probably best thawed first but can be cooked from frozen, using a meat thermometer to make certain the meat is properly cooked. It is absolutely essential that poultry and boned and rolled joints be completely thawed before cooking. Never try to hasten the thawing process by immersing in hot water.

COOKING METHODS

GRILLING – suitable for such small tender cuts as steaks, cutlets, chops, pork fillet, sausages, liver, kidney and poultry joints. Grilling has one major advantage: relatively little fat is required, making this an ideal cooking method for slimmers. A marinade will make the meat or poultry more juicy.

Preheat the grill until hot and brush grill rack with oil to prevent sticking. Brush both sides of meat with oil or butter. Grill the meat close to the heat for 1-2 minutes on each side, then lower the grill pan and continue cooking, turning and basting the meat every few minutes, until done to your liking.

Beef	Lamb	Pork	Offal	Poultry	Veal
fillet steak, rump steak, hamburgers: 7 mins rare 10 mins medium 12 mins well done	best end cutlets: 7-10 mins loin or chump chops: 10-15 mins shoulder chops: 12-15 mins	loin chops: 12-16 mins spare rib chops: 14-20 mins	kidneys: 8-10 mins	breasts and joints: 30-40 mins	cutlets and chops: 10-15 mins

FRYING – a fast method of cooking small pieces of tender meat, suited to steaks, chops and escalopes. Use a heavy-based frying pan and enough fat to cover the base of the pan to 3 mm (1/8 inch) for uncoated meats, 0.5 cm (1/4 inch) for meat coated in breadcrumbs. If the meat is uncoated dry with kitchen paper just before frying.

Stir-frying requires a wok or similar pan and the meat or poultry must be finely sliced; a good, quick way of 'stretching' meat and making a tasty dish.

Deep-frying is usually used for coated pieces of meat, poultry or fritters. A special deep-fat fryer with a basket makes the job easier and safer.

Beef	Lamb	Pork	Offal	Poultry	Veal
steaks and beef hamburgers: times as for grilling	chops and cutlets: times as for grilling	chops: times as for grilling	liver: 5-8 mins lambs kidneys: 6-8 mins calves kidneys: 8-10 mins	joints: 30-40 mins	escalopes: 5-6 mins

STEWING/CASSEROLING – long, slow cooking suitable for tougher cuts which can be cut into small pieces. The meat may or may not be browned first. Add enough liquid to barely cover, and flavourings, and simmer very gently on top of the cooker or in the oven at 160°C, 325°F, Gas Mark 3, until the meat is tender.

The cooking liquid can be wine, beer, cider, stock or water. When the stew is cooked the gravy will have absorbed the flavour of the meat, herbs and any vegetables included.

Beef	Lamb	Pork	Offal	Poultry	Veal
Braising cuts: 2½-3 hrs stewing cuts: 3½-4 hrs	shoulder meat: 1½-2 hrs stewing cuts: 2 hrs	hand: 2 hrs	oxtail: 3½-4 hrs	joints: 45 mins–1 hr	stewing cuts: 1½-2 hrs

ROASTING – use only the most tender joints for fast roasting at high temperatures (220°C, 425°F, Gas Mark 7). Small joints and less tender cuts of meat will shrink less and lose less moisture if you slow roast at 180°C, 350°F, Gas Mark 4. Place the weighed joint in a roasting tin, on a rack if you have one, with the thickest fat on top – if the joint is very lean, spread dripping on the top. Roast in a preheated oven for the calculated time (include the weight of any stuffing in the total weight), basting occasionally. The times below are a general guide only – joints on the bone will cook quicker than boneless cuts.

Beef	Lamb	Pork	Offal	Poultry	Veal
slow 25 mins per 450 g (1 lb) plus 25 mins – rare 30 mins per 450 g (1 lb) plus 30 mins – medium 35 mins per 450 g (1 lb) plus 35 mins – well done ***fast*** 15 mins per 450 g (1 lb) plus 15 mins – rare 20 mins per 450 g (1 lb) plus 20 mins – medium 25 mins per 450 g (1 lb) plus 25 mins – well done	***slow*** 30 mins per 450 g (1 lb) plus 30 mins ***fast*** 20 mins per 450 g (1 lb) plus 20 mins	***slow*** 35 mins per 450 g (1 lb) plus 30 mins ***fast*** 25 mins per 450 g (1 lb) plus 25 mins	hearts: can be stuffed and roasted in a slow oven	chicken: roast at 200°C, 400°F, Gas Mark 6 for 20 mins per 450 g (1 lb) plus 20 mins turkey: ***slow*** 2.75-4.5 kg (6-10 lb) 3-3¾ hrs 4.5-7.25 kg (10-16 lb) 3¾-4½ hrs 7.25-10 kg (16-22 lb) 4½-5¼ hrs ***fast*** 2.75-4.5 kg (6-10 lb) 2¼-2¾ hrs 4.5-7.25 kg (10-16 lb) 2¾-3¼ hrs 7.25-10 kg (16-22 lb) 3¼-4 hrs	***slow*** 30 mins per 450 g (1 lb) plus 30 mins ***fast*** 25 mins per 450 g (1 lb) plus 25 mins

BRAISING/POT ROASTING – a suitable method for less tender cuts. For pot roasting the joints are left whole and very little liquid is added; for braising the meat is cut into pieces. Brown the meat quickly in a flameproof casserole on top of the cooker, then add liquid and flavouring vegetables according to the recipe. Cover the casserole and cook slowly on top of the stove or brown the meat and vegetables in a frying pan, transfer to a casserole and cook in the oven at 160°C, 325°F, Gas Mark 3, until the meat is tender.

These are good-natured dishes that will not spoil if guests are late.

Beef	Lamb	Pork	Offal	Poultry	Veal
joints: 45 mins per 450 g (1 lb) with minimum of 2 hrs for topside, 3 hrs for silverside braising steak: 1½-2 hrs	joints: 40 mins per 450 g (1 lb) with minimum of 1½ hrs thick chops: 45 mins	fillet: 1 hr chops, spare ribs: 1½ hrs	hearts: 2 hrs	whole chicken: 1¼-2 hrs joints: 45 mins-1 hr	joints: 40 mins per 450 g (1 lb) with minimum of 1½ hrs

The most important requirements for good carving are a sharp carving knife, napkins, a carving fork and board or plate. It is best to serve the vegetables separately as putting them around the joint makes carving awkward.

Carving a loin of pork

1 Using a sharp knife cut a row of lines right through the pork skin at 5 mm (1/4 inch) intervals to prepare the crackling. Brush with oil and sprinkle with salt before roasting.

2 To carve, first turn the joint crackling side down to remove the chined bone.

3 Cut down along the edge of the bone towards the ribs so that the bone falls away from the meat.

4 Turn the joint crackling side up and carve in thin slices along the scored edge of the crackling. Cut the meat away from the ribs at the base of the joint.

Carving a leg of lamb

Carving a leg of lamb following these simple instructions will help you get the most economical use of this joint. Remember to use a clean napkin or cloth when holding the shank so as to improve your grasp and avoid burning yourself – you can use a carving fork to steady the joint for steps 1-3 if you prefer. Reserve the juices from the joint for the gravy.

1 Cut halfway along the length of the leg, pushing downwards until the blade reaches the bone. Make a second cut at an angle to the first to form a wedge shaped slice. Cut a few slices from either side to widen the 'V'.

2 Now carve thin slices from the centre towards the bone. Place all the slices on a heated serving dish. Gradually flatten the angle of the knife blade with each slice to get larger slices of meat.

3 When all the meat has been carved from one end return to the centre of the joint and repeat the process carving away from the shank with the knife blade angled towards you.

4 When all the meat has been removed, turn the joint over, lifting it slightly and resting it on the carving dish. Carve with the knife blade at a shallow angle until all the remaining meat has been sliced off cleanly.

Beef with celery and walnuts

SERVES 4

2 tbls vegetable oil
450 g (1 lb) braising steak, trimmed and cut into 2.5 cm (1 inch) cubes
15 g (½ oz) margarine or butter
2 onions, chopped
1 carrot, diced
1 tbls plain flour
300 ml (½ pint) beef stock
salt and pepper
4 stalks celery, sliced into 2.5 cm (1 inch) lengths
½ tsp dried mixed herbs
1 tbls soured cream
50 g (2 oz) walnuts, chopped

Heat the oven to 150°C, 300°F, Gas Mark 2. Heat the oil in a large frying pan, add the beef and fry over moderately high heat, turning occasionally, for 3-4 minutes, to seal and brown evenly. Remove to a medium casserole.

Melt the margarine or butter in the frying pan, add the onions and carrot, and fry gently for 5 minutes until softened. Sprinkle in the flour and cook for a further 1-2 minutes, stirring constantly, then gradually add the stock, stirring to make a smooth sauce.

Season well and pour over the meat. Stir in the celery and herbs. Cover and cook in the oven for 1½-1¾ hours, or until the beef is tender.

Just before serving, taste and adjust the seasoning, swirl the soured cream over the top and sprinkle with the nuts.

Carbonnade of beef

SERVES 4

2 tbls vegetable oil
1 kg (2 lb) chuck steak, trimmed and cut into 2.5 cm (1 inch) cubes
25 g (1 oz) plain flour, seasoned with salt and pepper
2 large onions, finely chopped
300 ml (½ pint) sweet stout
1 tsp wine vinegar
1 bouquet garni
salt and freshly ground black pepper
1 tbls chopped fresh parsley, to garnish

Heat the oven to 160°C, 325°F, Gas Mark 3. Heat the oil in a medium flameproof casserole. Toss the meat cubes in the seasoned flour to coat. Add the beef to the casserole and fry over a high heat, turning frequently, for 2-3 minutes, until evenly brown. Remove the meat with a slotted spoon and set aside on a plate.

Add the onions to the casserole and fry gently for 5-10 minutes until lightly browned. Return the meat to the casserole and stir in the stout, vinegar and bouquet garni. Season well with salt and plenty of freshly ground pepper. Heat until simmering, then cover and cook in the oven for 2-2½ hours, or until the meat is tender. Check the casserole during cooking and stir in a little water if it shows signs of becoming dry.

Remove the bouquet garni and adjust the seasoning to taste. Sprinkle with the parsley and serve at once.

Variation: Replace 1 onion with 4 chopped celery stalks and 2 sliced carrots, to give a mixture of vegetables. Or cover the top of the casserole with slices of French bread spread with mustard for the last 10 minutes of cooking.

Serving ideas: Serve with creamed potatoes and braised red cabbage.

• Beef with celery and walnuts; Carbonnade of beef

Rich chicken casserole

SERVES 4

2 tbls vegetable oil
4 chicken joints
2 large onions, sliced
1 carrot, diced
2 rashers streaky bacon, rinded and chopped
salt and pepper
6 tbls red wine
300 ml (½ pint) boiling chicken stock
1 bouquet garni
1 bay leaf
6 button onions, peeled
40 g (1½ oz) margarine or butter
4 button mushrooms, thinly sliced
2 tbls plain flour
2 tbls single cream
1 tbls chopped fresh parsley, to garnish

Heat the oven to 160°C, 325°F, Gas Mark 3. Heat the oil in a large frying pan, add the chicken joints and fry over moderate heat for about 5 minutes, turning once, until the chicken is golden. Remove the chicken joints and place in a shallow casserole.

Add the onions, carrot and bacon to the frying pan and fry gently for 5 minutes until softened. Place on top of the chicken, season and add 4 tbls of the wine, the stock, bouquet garni and bay leaf. Cover the casserole and cook in the oven for 1 hour.

Heat the remaining wine in a small saucepan, add the button onions and simmer gently for 10 minutes, or until the onions are tender. Remove the onions and set aside, reserving the wine.

Melt 15 g (½ oz) of the margarine in a small frying pan, add the mushrooms and fry gently for 2-3 minutes until softened. Remove the mushrooms and set aside.

Melt the remaining fat in a small saucepan, sprinkle in the flour and cook for 1-2 minutes over a low heat, stirring. Add the wine from the onions and about 6 tbls stock from the casserole to make a thin, smooth sauce. Stir into the casserole, along with the onions and mushrooms. Cook in the oven for a further 15 minutes or until the chicken is tender.

Remove the bouquet garni and bay leaf and adjust the seasoning to taste. Stir in the cream, sprinkle with the parsley and serve at once.

Chicken Madras

SERVES 4

50 g (2 oz) margarine or butter
1.5 kg (3 lb) chicken, jointed
2 onions, chopped
2 tbls hot curry powder
2 garlic cloves, chopped
900 ml (1½ pints) chicken stock
25 ml (1 fl oz) lemon juice
2 tbls tomato purée
1 tbls demerara sugar
2 bay leaves
salt and pepper
1 hard-boiled egg, cut into wedges, to garnish

Melt the fat in a large heavy-based saucepan or flameproof casserole. Add the chicken pieces, onions and curry powder and fry over a moderate heat, turning occasionally, for 5 minutes, or until the chicken has evenly browned. Add the garlic, stock, lemon juice, tomato purée, sugar, bay leaves and seasoning. Bring to the boil, then cover, lower the heat and simmer for 1½ hours or until the chicken is tender.

Remove the bay leaves and adjust the seasoning to taste. Transfer to a heated serving dish, arrange the egg wedges over the top, and serve.

Serving ideas: Serve with plain boiled rice and a selection of side dishes, such as mango chutney, desiccated coconut, sliced banana, cucumber and yoghurt.

• Top: Rich chicken casserole
Bottom: Chicken Madras

Lamb and leek casserole

SERVES 4

750 g (1½ lb) middle or best end neck of lamb, trimmed and cut into cutlets
50 g (2 oz) plain flour, seasoned
25 g (1 oz) margarine or butter
3 medium leeks, sliced into rounds
397 g (14 oz) can tomatoes, drained, juice reserved
300 ml (½ pint) water or chicken stock
1 tbls tomato purée
½ tsp dried thyme
2 tsp dried mixed herbs
salt and pepper
parsley sprigs, to garnish

• Left: Lancashire hot pot
Right: Lamb and leek casserole

Heat the oven to 160°C, 325°F, Gas Mark 3. Toss the cutlets in the seasoned flour reserving any excess. Melt the fat in a large frying pan, add the cutlets and fry over moderate heat, turning occasionally, for 3-4 minutes until evenly brown. Transfer lamb to casserole.

Add the leeks to the pan and fry gently for 2 minutes until softened. Remove with a slotted spoon and add to the casserole together with the tomatoes.

Sprinkle the remaining seasoned flour into the fat in the frying pan and cook for 1-2 minutes, stirring constantly. Add the water or stock, the reserved tomato juice, tomato purée, herbs and seasoning. Bring gently to the boil, stirring. Pour over the lamb in the casserole, cover and cook for 2 hours or until the lamb is tender.

Adjust the seasoning to taste, garnish with parsley sprigs and serve.

Serving idea: Serve with potatoes.

Lancashire hot pot

SERVES 4

750g (1½lb) best end neck of lamb, trimmed and cut into cutlets
50g (2oz) plain flour, seasoned
2 tbls dripping
4 lambs' kidneys, skinned, cored and halved
3 onions, sliced
3 carrots, sliced
4 potatoes, sliced
450 ml (¾ pint) chicken stock
sprig of fresh thyme or pinch of dried thyme
½ tsp Worcestershire sauce
salt and pepper
2 tbls chopped fresh parsley, to garnish

Heat the oven to 160°C, 325°F, Gas Mark 3. Toss the cutlets in the seasoned flour, reserving any excess. Melt the dripping in a large frying pan, add the cutlets and fry over moderate heat, turning occasionally, for 3-4 minutes until evenly brown. Remove from the pan and place in a casserole. Add the kidneys to the casserole.

Reduce the heat and add the onions and carrots to the pan. Fry gently for 5 minutes until softened. Remove with a slotted spoon and add to the casserole. Arrange the potato slices over the top.

Sprinkle the remaining seasoned flour into the fat in the frying pan and cook, stirring constantly, for 1-2 minutes. Stir in the stock and bring to the boil. Add the thyme and Worcestershire sauce, and adjust the seasoning to taste. Pour over the potatoes, cover and cook in the oven for 1½ hours.

Remove the lid and baste the potatoes with a little of the gravy. Return to the oven and continue to cook, uncovered, for about 40 minutes, until the potatoes are tender and brown. Sprinkle the potato topping with chopped parsley and serve.

Oxtail casserole

SERVES 6

2 tbls vegetable oil
2 oxtails, cut into 5 cm (2 inch) pieces
2 onions, sliced
2 carrots, sliced
1 garlic clove, crushed
2 tbls tomato purée
300 ml (1/2 pint) boiling beef stock
150 ml (1/4 pint) sherry
salt and pepper
bouquet garni
25 g (1 oz) margarine or butter
450 g (1 lb) button onions
100 g (4 oz) button mushrooms

Heat the oven to 160°C, 325°F, Gas Mark 3. Heat the oil in a large frying pan, add the oxtail and fry over moderate heat, turning occasionally, for 3-4 minutes until evenly brown. Transfer the oxtail to a flameproof casserole.

Reduce the heat, add the vegetables and garlic and fry for 5 minutes until softened. Place on top of the oxtail. Blend together the tomato purée, stock and sherry, and pour over the contents of the casserole. Season and add the bouquet garni. Cover and cook in the oven for about 3 hours, until the meat is tender and falling off the bones.

Remove the bouquet garni. Lift the oxtail pieces from the casserole and remove the meat from the bones and reserve. Set the casserole aside, to cool.

Meanwhile, melt the margarine in a small frying pan, add the button onions and fry gently for 10 minutes until brown. Add the mushrooms and cook for 5 minutes, until the vegetables are softened.

Skim the fat from the surface of the cooled casserole and add the meat, onions and mushrooms. Bring to the boil on top of the cooker, cover and simmer gently for 10 minutes.

Taste and adjust the seasoning, garnish with the parsley sprigs and serve.

Rabbit casserole

SERVES 4

1.5 kg (3 lb) rabbit, cut into joints
2 tbls plain flour, seasoned
50 g (2 oz) bacon, rinded and chopped
25 g (1 oz) margarine or butter
1 tbls vegetable oil
12 button onions
2 celery stalks, sliced
1 red pepper, cored, seeded and cut into strips
4 tbls white wine
150 ml (1/4 pint) boiling chicken stock
1/2 tsp dried rosemary
salt and pepper
rosemary sprigs, to garnish
For the beurre manié
15 g (1/2 oz) butter
15 g (1/2 oz) plain flour

Heat the oven to 150°C, 300°F, Gas Mark 2. Toss the rabbit pieces in the seasoned flour. Fry the bacon in a large frying pan in the margarine and oil for 5 minutes until lightly browned. Transfer to a flameproof casserole.

Increase the heat, add the rabbit joints and fry, turning occasionally, for 3-4 minutes until evenly brown. Transfer to the casserole. Reduce the heat, add the onions to the pan and fry for about 5 minutes until golden brown. Add to the casserole. Fry the celery and pepper gently for 5 minutes until softened, then add to the casserole.

Pour the wine and stock into the casserole, stir in the rosemary and season. Cover and cook in the oven for 1 hour, or until the rabbit is tender.

Transfer the rabbit and onions to a heated serving dish and put the casserole over low heat. Smoothly blend the butter and flour for the beurre manié. Gradually add small pieces to the sauce in the casserole, whisking well between each addition until the sauce is smooth and thick. Pour over the rabbit, garnish with rosemary and serve.

• **Top: Rabbit casserole; Bottom: Oxtail casserole**

• Pork chops in ginger beer; Curried pork

Curried pork

SERVES 4

3 tbls vegetable oil
1 tbls coriander seeds
1 tbls cumin seeds
1 tbls sesame seeds
4 cloves
750 g (1½ lb) pork fillet, cut into 2.5 cm (1 inch) cubes
1 tbls ground turmeric
2 tbls soft light brown sugar
150 ml (¼ pint) wine vinegar
150 ml (¼ pint) chicken stock or water
salt and pepper
To garnish
lemon wedges
fresh coriander sprigs

Heat the oven to 150°C, 300°F, Gas Mark 2. Heat the oil in a large flameproof casserole. Add the coriander, cumin, sesame seeds and cloves and fry over moderate heat, stirring, for 2 minutes. Add the pork and fry for a further 3-4 minutes, turning occasionally, until the meat is lightly browned. Add the turmeric and cook for 1 minute. Stir in the sugar, vinegar and stock and season to taste.

Bring slowly to the boil, cover and cook in the oven for 1½ hours, or until the pork is tender. If the dish shows signs of drying out during cooking, add a little extra stock as required.

To serve, transfer to a heated serving dish and garnish with lemon wedges and coriander sprigs.

Serving ideas: Serve with pilau rice and a bowl of chilled yoghurt, with small dishes of chopped onion, chopped green pepper, tomato wedges and mango chutney. Garnish with toasted cashew nuts.

Pork chops in ginger beer

SERVES 4

25 g (1 oz) margarine or butter
4 pork chops, trimmed
1 large onion, sliced into rings
2 celery stalks, chopped
2 carrots, thinly sliced
25 g (1 oz) plain flour
450 ml (3/4 pint) ginger beer
1 beef stock cube dissolved in 4 tbls hot water
a few drops of Worcestershire or Tabasco sauce
25 ml (1 fl oz) lemon juice
225 g (8 oz) tomatoes, skinned, seeded and chopped
salt and pepper

Heat the oven to 180°C, 350°F, Gas Mark 4. Melt the margarine in a large frying pan, add the chops and fry over a moderate heat, turning once, for 3-4 minutes until brown on each side. Remove the chops from the pan and arrange them in a single layer in a shallow heatproof casserole.

Reduce the heat, add the onion, celery and carrots, and fry gently for 5 minutes until soft. Sprinkle on the flour and cook, stirring, for 1 minute. Gradually stir in the ginger beer and stock and bring to the boil, stirring constantly, to make a smooth sauce. Stir in the Worcestershire sauce, lemon juice, tomatoes, salt and plenty of freshly ground black pepper.

Pour the sauce over the chops, cover the casserole and cook in the oven for 45 minutes or until the pork is tender. Adjust the seasoning to taste before serving.

Serving ideas: Serve with steamed new potatoes, lightly buttered and tossed in finely chopped parsley and lightly cooked broccoli spears or French beans, sprinkled with lemon juice or olive oil.

Casseroled sausages

SERVES 4

4 large herb-flavoured pork sausages
4 thick bacon rashers, rinded
25 g (1 oz) margarine or butter
2 tbls vegetable oil
1 onion, chopped
1½ tsp dried sage
1½ tbls plain flour
450 ml (¾ pint) chicken stock
salt and pepper
142 ml (5 fl oz) carton soured cream
2 tbls chopped fresh parsley, to garnish

Wrap each sausage in a bacon rasher and secure with fine string. Heat the margarine and oil in a medium flameproof casserole, add the onion and fry gently for 5 minutes until softened. Add the sage and the wrapped sausages and fry for a further 5 minutes, turning occasionally, until the bacon is browned. Remove the sausages and set aside.

Sprinkle the flour into the casserole and cook, stirring, for 1 minute. Gradually stir in the stock. Bring to the boil, then season and stir in the soured cream. Return the sausages to the casserole, cover and simmer gently for 20 minutes until tender.

Sprinkle with the parsley and serve.

Serving ideas: Serve the sausages with their sauce on a bed of buttered noodles, accompanied by a crisp green salad.

Variation: Use cider instead of chicken stock to give this dish a special flavour.

• Right: Hungarian veal goulash
Bottom: Casseroled sausages

Hungarian veal goulash

SERVES 4-6

25g (1 oz) dripping or lard
1 large onion, finely chopped
1 garlic clove, crushed
1 kg (2 lb) pie veal, trimmed and cut into 2.5 cm (1 inch) cubes
½ tsp caraway seeds
2 tbls paprika
1 tsp dried mixed herbs
salt and pepper
1 red pepper, cored, seeded and sliced into rings
1 green pepper, cored, seeded and sliced into rings
397 g (14 oz) can tomatoes
150 ml (¼ pint) chicken stock
225 g (8 oz) button mushrooms, sliced
142 ml (5 fl oz) carton soured cream
1 tbls chopped fresh parsley, to garnish

Heat the oven to 150°C, 300°F, Gas Mark 2. Melt the fat in a flameproof casserole, add the onion and garlic and fry gently for 5 minutes until soft. Increase the heat, add the veal and fry quickly, turning, until evenly brown.

Stir in the caraway seeds, paprika, herbs and seasoning to taste. Cook for a further 1-2 minutes, stirring constantly, then add the peppers, tomatoes with their juice and stock. Bring to simmering point, then cover and cook in the oven for 1½ hours.

Add the mushrooms to the casserole and cook in the oven for a further 30 minutes or until the veal is tender.

Adjust the seasoning to taste, then swirl the soured cream over the top of the casserole and sprinkle with the parsley. Serve immediately.

Serving ideas: Serve with buttered noodles and a green salad.

Roast beef and Yorkshire pudding

SERVES 4-6

40g (1½oz) dripping or lard
1-1.25kg (2-2½lb) boned rolled sirloin
1 tbls plain flour
salt and pepper
300ml (½pint) beef stock
For the Yorkshire pudding
50g (2oz) plain flour
¼tsp salt
100ml (3½fl oz) milk
50ml (2fl oz) water
1 egg

Heat the oven to 180°C, 350°F, Gas Mark 4. Put the fat in a roasting tin and place in the oven until melted.

Weigh the joint and calculate the cooking time at 20 minutes per 450g (1lb), plus 20 minutes. Pat dry with absorbent paper. Season the flour with salt and pepper and rub over the cut surfaces of the meat. Place the meat in the roasting tin and roast in the oven for the calculated cooking time.

Meanwhile, make the Yorkshire pudding batter. Sift the flour with the salt into a mixing bowl and make a well in the centre. Combine the milk with the water. Place the egg in the well, add half the milk and water, and with a small wire whisk gradually draw the flour into the liquid and beat until smooth. Beat in the remaining milk and water, cover and chill the batter in the refrigerator until required.

When the beef is cooked transfer it to a heated carving dish, remove the string and leave in a warm place to rest for 15 minutes. Raise the oven heat to 220°C, 425°F, Gas Mark 7.

Pour a little of the hot fat from the roasting tin into each of 4 large bun tins; divide the batter between them. Cook for 20 minutes until risen and golden.

Meanwhile, drain off any excess fat from the roasting tin. Place the roasting tin on top of the stove over a low heat, add the stock, stir to mix with the pan juices and simmer gently for 5 minutes. Pour into a heated gravy boat.

Arrange the Yorkshire puddings around the beef. Carve beef into slices and serve with the gravy.

• Left: Pot-roasted beef
Right: Roast beef and Yorkshire pudding

Pot-roasted beef

SERVES 4-6

15 g (½ oz) beef dripping or lard
salt and pepper
1-1.25 kg (2-2½ lb) piece of brisket or topside of beef, trimmed
1 large onion, finely chopped
1 garlic clove, crushed
397 g (14 oz) can tomatoes
100 g (4 oz) green or black olives, stoned
150 ml (¼ pint) dry white wine
1 tsp chopped fresh thyme or ½ tsp dried thyme

Heat the oven to 180°C, 350°F, Gas Mark 4. Melt the dripping or lard in a large flameproof casserole. Season the beef, place in the casserole and fry quickly over a high heat, turning, until browned on all sides. Remove from the casserole and set aside.

Reduce the heat, add the onion and garlic and fry gently for 2-3 minutes until golden. Return the beef to the casserole and add the tomatoes with their juice, the olives, white wine and the fresh or dried thyme.

Cover and cook in the oven for 2-2½ hours or until the meat is very tender, adding a little water if necessary.

Transfer the meat to a heated serving platter and carve into thick slices. Adjust the seasoning of the sauce to taste, spoon a little over the meat slices and hand the remaining sauce separately in a heated gravy boat.

Variation: For a heartier dish, replace the chopped onion with 12 button onions, and 450 g (1 lb) mixed root vegetables (carrots, turnips, swede), cut into chunks. Omit the tomatoes and olives.

• French roast chicken; Honey roast duckling salad

French roast chicken

SERVES 4-6

1.5-1.75 kg (3-4 lb) roasting chicken
65 g (2½ oz) butter, softened
2 tbls chopped fresh mixture of parsley, tarragon, chervil, as available
1 garlic clove, crushed
salt and pepper
squeeze of lemon juice
watercress sprigs, to garnish

Heat the oven to 190°C, 375°F, Gas Mark 5. Remove the chicken giblets and reserve for making stock. Weigh the bird and calculate the cooking time at 20 minutes per 450 g (1 lb) plus 20 minutes. Wash the chicken under cold water and dry with absorbent paper.

Cream half of the butter with the herbs and garlic, and season well. Place the mixture in the cavity of the chicken. Tie the legs together with fine string.

Lay the bird on its side in a roasting tin and spread with half the remaining butter. Cook in the oven for one-third of the calculated time.

Turn the bird on its other side, spread with the remaining butter and cook for a further one-third of the calculated time. Then turn the bird breast up, baste with the pan juices and complete cooking until the chicken is tender, and the juices run clear when the thickest part of the thigh is pierced with a metal skewer.

Lift the bird from the tin and place on a heated carving dish. Remove the string and keep warm while making the gravy. Drain the excess fat from the pan. Add a squeeze of lemon juice to the pan juices, reheat gently on top of the stove, stirring, then pour into a heated gravy boat.

Garnish the chicken with the watercress and serve the gravy separately.

Honey roast duckling salad

SERVES 4

2.25-2.75 kg (5-6 lb) duckling
salt and pepper
1 small onion
2 tbls clear honey
1 tbls boiling water
For the salad
4-6 crisp lettuce leaves
2 large oranges, peeled and thinly sliced into rounds
1 small pineapple, peeled, cored and sliced into rings, or 227 g (8 oz) can pineapple rings, drained
8 black or green olives
watercress sprigs
6 tbls French dressing

Heat the oven to 180°C, 350°F, Gas Mark 4. Remove the giblets from the duckling and reserve for making stock. Weigh the bird and calculate the cooking time at 30 minutes per 450 g (1 lb).

Rinse the duckling under cold running water and pat dry with absorbent paper. Prick the skin all over with a fork. Sprinkle the body cavity with salt and pepper and insert the onion.

Place the bird breast upwards on a rack in a roasting tin and sprinkle with salt. Roast in the oven for 1 hour.

Drain off the fat from the roasting tin. Blend the honey with the boiling water and spoon over the surface of the duck. Cook for the remaining calculated time, basting occasionally with the pan juices, until the duckling is tender and the juices run clear when the thigh is pierced with a skewer.

Remove the duckling from the oven and leave for at least 4 hours, or until cold. Cut into 4 serving portions.

To serve, arrange the duckling portions in the centre of a serving platter on a bed of lettuce. Arrange the orange and pineapple slices around the edge. Place an olive in the centre of each pineapple and orange slice; garnish with the watercress. Sprinkle salad ingredients with French dressing.

French roast leg of lamb

SERVES 4-6

1.5-2 kg (3-4 lb) leg of lamb
1 garlic clove, cut into slivers
25 g (1 oz) dripping or lard, melted
salt and pepper
1 carrot, sliced
1 onion, quartered
300 ml (½ pint) beef stock
rosemary sprigs, to garnish

Heat the oven to 230°C, 450°F, Gas Mark 8. Pat the lamb dry with absorbent paper. Using a sharp knife, make several incisions in the joint and insert a garlic sliver into each. Brush the lamb with the melted dripping and sprinkle with salt and pepper.

Place the joint on a rack in a roasting tin and roast on the top shelf of the oven for 15-20 minutes, basting occasionally, until the lamb is browned.

Place the carrot and onion in the roasting tin under the rack, and transfer to the centre shelf of the oven. Reduce the heat to 180°C, 350°F, Gas Mark 4, and roast for 1-1½ hours, or until the juices run rosy pink when the lamb is pierced with a skewer.

Transfer the lamb to a heated serving dish and keep warm. Drain off the excess fat from the pan and mash the vegetables with a fork. Pour in the beef stock and bring to the boil over high heat, stirring constantly to mix the meat juices into the gravy. Season to taste and pour into a heated gravy boat.

Serve the lamb carved into slices, garnished with rosemary sprigs, with the gravy handed separately.

Serving ideas: Serve with potatoes boulangère (sliced into a dish, covered with stock and baked in the oven) and courgettes.
Variation: For a special occasion, replace half the stock with 150 ml (¼ pint) red wine.

• French roast leg of lamb; Crown roast of lamb; Stuffed breast of lamb

Stuffed breast of lamb

SERVES 4

1 kg (2½ lb) boned breast of lamb
salt and pepper
1 tbls plain flour
300 ml (½ pint) beef stock
For the stuffing
50 g (2 oz) can anchovy fillets, drained and soaked in milk for 30 minutes, then drained and finely chopped
75 g (3 oz) fresh white breadcrumbs
1 small onion, finely chopped
100 g (4 oz) mushrooms, chopped
1 tbls chopped fresh parsley
about ½ egg, beaten

Heat the oven to 190°C, 375°F, Gas Mark 5. Lay the lamb flat and season.

Put all the stuffing ingredients except the egg in a bowl. Stir well, then mix in enough egg to bind. Season to taste.

Spread the stuffing over the breast. Roll up carefully and tie in several places with fine string. Place on a rack in a roasting tin, season lightly and roast for 1½-2 hours, until the meat is tender and the outside skin is crisp.

Transfer to a heated serving platter, remove the string and keep warm while making the gravy. Drain excess fat from roasting tin, then set tin over a low heat and stir in the flour. Cook for 1-2 minutes, then gradually add the stock, stirring, to make a smooth gravy. Bring to simmering point, season and pour into a gravy boat.

To serve, remove the string and skewers and carve the lamb into slices.

Crown roast of lamb

SERVES 4-6

1 crown roast of lamb (2 best ends of lamb with 4-6 cutlets each), prepared by the butcher
mint sprigs, to garnish

For the stuffing

15 g (½ oz) margarine or butter
1 small onion, finely chopped
2 celery stalks, finely chopped
175 g (6 oz) fresh white breadcrumbs
2 tbls chopped fresh mint
2 tbls lemon juice
salt and pepper
1 egg, beaten

Heat the oven to 180°C, 350°F, Gas Mark 4. To make the stuffing, melt the margarine in a small saucepan. Add the onion and celery and fry gently for 5 minutes until soft. Transfer to a mixing bowl and stir in the breadcrumbs, mint, lemon juice and seasoning. Stir in the egg to bind.

Weigh the crown roast and calculate the cooking time at 25 minutes per 450 g (1 lb) plus 25 minutes. Place in a roasting tin. Spoon the stuffing into the centre of the crown roast. Cover the ends of the cutlet bones and the stuffing with foil.

Roast in the oven for the calculated time, until the meat at the base of the cutlets is tender when pierced with a skewer.

Remove from the roasting tin and place on a heated serving dish. Remove the foil and decorate the cutlet bones with cutlet frills. Garnish with mint sprigs around the base of the roast and serve immediately.

Variation: Omit the stuffing and pile lightly cooked spring vegetables such as mangetout and baby carrots into the centre of the crown to serve.

Roast loin of pork with apples and prunes

SERVES 4

1 kg (2¼ lb) loin of pork, boned, skinned, rolled and tied
1 small cooking apple, peeled, cored and chopped
8 prunes, stoned and chopped
25 g (1 oz) margarine or butter
150 ml (¼ pint) dry cider
150 ml (¼ pint) chicken stock
salt and pepper
2 tbls clear honey
1 tbls French mustard
1 tbls plain flour

Heat the oven to 180°C, 350°F, Gas Mark 4. Using a sharpening steel, make a hole through the 'eye' of the pork.

Mix together the apple and prunes and stuff the hole with the mixture.

Melt the margarine in a large frying pan, add the pork and fry over a moderately high heat, turning occasionally, for 3-4 minutes until evenly brown.

Transfer the pork to a roasting tin, fat side up, and pour over the cider and stock. Season, then cover the tin with foil and cook in the oven for 1 hour.

Remove the tin from the oven, remove the foil and pour off and reserve nearly all the pan juices, leaving enough to just cover the bottom of the tin. Mix together the honey and mustard and brush over the pork. Raise the oven heat to 200°C, 400°F, Gas Mark 6. Cook the pork, uncovered, for a further 30 minutes or until tender.

Remove the pork from the oven and keep warm. Place the roasting tin over gentle heat, stir in the flour and cook, stirring, for 2-3 minutes. Pour in the reserved juices and stir well to mix. Bring to the boil, cook for 2-3 minutes, then strain into a heated sauceboat.

Remove the string from the pork, carve into thick slices and arrange on a heated serving dish. Serve with the sauce handed separately.

Serving idea: Serve with sauté potatoes.

Traditional English roast turkey

SERVES 8-12

5-6 kg (10-12 lb) turkey
50 g (2 oz) dripping or butter, melted
salt and pepper
For the forcemeat
100 g (4 oz) margarine or butter, melted
225 g (8 oz) fresh white breadcrumbs
4 tbls chopped fresh parsley
1 tbls chopped fresh thyme
grated rind of 1 lemon
1-2 eggs, beaten
For the chestnut and sausage stuffing
435 g (1 lb) can puréed unsweetened chestnuts
750 g (1½ lb) pork sausagemeat
1 onion, chopped
1 tsp mixed spice
1-2 tbls brandy
For the gravy
turkey giblets
1 carrot, sliced
1 onion, sliced
1 bay leaf
2 tbls plain flour
To garnish
chipolata sausages, fried or grilled
bacon rolls, fried or grilled

Heat the oven to 160°C, 325°F, Gas Mark 3. Wash the turkey and pat dry with absorbent paper.

For the forcemeat, place all the ingredients except the egg in a large bowl and mix well. Stir in enough egg to bind.

For the chestnut and sausage stuffing, place all the ingredients except the brandy in a large bowl and mix well. Stir in enough brandy to moisten.

Spoon the forcemeat into the neck end of the turkey and the chestnut and sausage stuffing into the body cavity. Sew up both openings with trussing string, securing with skewers if necessary. Weigh the stuffed bird and calculate the cooking time at 15 minutes per 450 g (1 lb), plus 15 minutes.

Brush the turkey with the dripping

and season well. Place on a rack in a roasting tin and cover loosely with foil. Roast for the calculated cooking time, basting and turning occasionally. Remove the foil for the last 15 minutes to brown the skin. To test if the bird is cooked, pierce the thigh with a skewer; it is done when the juices run clear.

Meanwhile, prepare the gravy. Put the giblets, except for the liver, into a saucepan and cover with water. Add the carrot, onion, bay leaf and season to taste. Bring to the boil, then reduce the heat, cover and simmer for 1 hour. Strain into a measuring jug and make up to 600 ml (1 pint) with the cooking water from the vegetables.

Remove the turkey from the oven and transfer to a heated serving platter. Remove the string and skewers; keep warm.

Drain the excess fat from the roasting tin. Place over a moderate heat and stir in the flour. Cook for 1-2 minutes, stirring constantly, then gradually stir in the giblet stock. Bring to the boil, then simmer gently for 1-2 minutes. Pour into a heated gravy boat.

Serve the turkey garnished with chipolatas and bacon rolls, with the gravy.

• Traditional English roast turkey; Roast loin of pork with apples and prunes

• Glazed baked gammon

Glazed baked gammon

SERVES 4

1.5 kg (3 lb) gammon joint, soaked in cold water overnight
6 whole black peppercorns
6 juniper berries (optional)
1 bay leaf
1 onion, studded with a few cloves
2 tbls clear honey
To garnish
about 50 cloves
4 canned pineapple rings, fried in butter and a little soft light brown sugar
watercress sprigs

Drain the gammon and calculate the cooking time at 30 minutes per 450 g (1 lb). Place in a large saucepan with the peppercorns, juniper berries, if using, bay leaf and onion. Cover with cold water and bring to the boil, skimming well with a slotted spoon. Reduce the heat, cover and simmer gently for the calculated cooking time.

Remove the gammon from the pan and allow to cool slightly. Heat the oven to 200°C, 400°F, Gas Mark 6. Remove the rind and some of the fat from the joint. Score the remaining fat surface in a diamond pattern with a sharp knife, then brush with the honey.

Place the gammon on a rack in a roasting tin and bake in the oven for 15-20 minutes until glazed and crisp.

Transfer to a heated serving platter and stud each diamond with a clove. Serve carved into slices, garnished with the fried pineapple slices and watercress sprigs.

Serving ideas: Serve with baked potatoes and broad beans in a parsley sauce and a fresh green salad.

Beef and peanut burgers

SERVES 4

75g (3oz) salted peanuts
450g (1 lb) lean minced beef
1 onion, chopped
salt and pepper
1 egg, beaten
2 tbls vegetable oil
4 baps
2 tomatoes, sliced
lettuce leaves, to garnish

Reserve a few peanuts for the garnish and chop the remainder. Place the chopped peanuts in a large bowl with the mince, onion and seasoning to taste. Mix well, then stir in the beaten egg to bind. Divide the mixture into 4 equal portions and shape each one into a flat round burger.

Heat the oil in a large frying pan. Add the burgers and fry over a moderate heat for 10 minutes, turning occasionally, or until lightly browned and cooked through.

Meanwhile, warm the baps. Split in half and place a burger in each, topped with tomato slices and a few peanuts.

To serve, place the baps on a bed of lettuce on a serving dish.

Serving ideas: Serve with a green salad dressed with blue cheese dressing, accompanied by hamburger relish.
Variation: Use 100g (4oz) chopped mushrooms instead of the peanuts.

• **Beef and peanut burgers**

Bobotie

SERVES 4

3 tbls vegetable oil
1 large onion, finely chopped
450 g (1 lb) minced beef
2 tsp mild curry powder
½ tsp ground turmeric
1 tbls wine vinegar
150 ml (¼ pint) beef stock
2 tomatoes, peeled and chopped
salt
1 large slice white or brown bread, soaked in milk
25 g (1 oz) chopped almonds
50 g (2 oz) sultanas
1 tbls soft light brown sugar
1 tbls apricot jam or mango chutney
2 eggs, beaten
300 ml (½ pint) milk
4 fresh bay leaves
lemon slices, to garnish

Heat the oil in a large frying pan, add the onion and fry gently for 7 minutes until golden. Add the mince and cook, stirring, until brown.

Blend the curry powder and turmeric with the vinegar and stir into the mince mixture. Add the stock, tomatoes and salt and cook gently, uncovered, for 15 minutes. Heat the oven to 180°C, 350°F, Gas Mark 4.

Drain the bread from the milk. Cut into small pieces and stir into the mince mixture together with the almonds, sultanas, sugar and apricot jam or mango chutney.

Spoon into a shallow greased ovenproof dish. Place the dish in the oven and bake for 30 minutes.

Beat the eggs with the milk and add a little salt. Strain over the mince mixture, and arrange the bay leaves on top.

Return to the oven for a further 30 minutes, or until the custard is set. Garnish with the lemon slices and serve immediately.

Serving ideas: Serve with boiled rice and a mixed salad.

Country beef and potato pie

SERVES 4-6

1 tbls vegetable oil
1 large onion, finely chopped
1 large celery stalk, finely chopped
750 g (1½ lb) minced beef
1 tbls plain flour
2 tbls tomato purée
150 ml (¼ pint) brown ale or beer
1 bay leaf
salt and pepper
For the topping
450 g (1 lb) potatoes
225 g (8 oz) parsnips
3 tbls milk
40 g (1½ oz) margarine or butter

Heat the oil in a medium frying pan, add the onion and celery and fry gently for 5 minutes until soft. Add the mince and cook, stirring, until brown.

Stir in the flour and cook for 1 minute. Add the tomato purée, ale or beer, and the bay leaf. Season, then bring to the boil. Reduce the heat, cover the pan, and simmer for 30 minutes, stirring occasionally.

Meanwhile, prepare the topping. Cook the potatoes and parsnips in boiling salted water until tender. Drain the vegetables, place in a large mixing bowl, and mash together smoothly. Add the milk, 25 g (1 oz) of the butter and seasoning to taste, and mix well. Heat the oven to 180°C, 350°F, Gas Mark 4.

Turn the mince mixture into a shallow 1.5 litre (2½ pint) ovenproof dish. Pipe over or cover with the vegetable topping and then mark decoratively with a fork. Melt the remaining butter and brush over the top. Bake in the oven for 45 minutes or until the topping is golden brown.

Serving ideas: Serve with a green vegetable such as sprouts or buttered cabbage.

• **Top: Country beef and potato pie**
Bottom: Bobotie

Gingered beef patties

SERVES 4

450g (1 lb) minced beef
1 onion, finely chopped
50g (2 oz) fresh brown or white breadcrumbs
1 egg, beaten
2 tbls chopped fresh parsley
salt and pepper
2 tbls vegetable oil
300 ml (½ pint) boiling beef stock
1 tbls dark brown sugar
1 tsp ground ginger
50g (2 oz) seedless raisins
50 ml (2 fl oz) lemon juice
25g (1 oz) margarine or butter
8 pineapple rings, fresh or canned
2 tsp arrowroot
2 tbls cold water
To garnish
lemon twists
4 pieces stem ginger, sliced

Heat the oven to 180°C, 350°F, Gas Mark 4. Place the mince, onion, breadcrumbs, egg and parsley in a large mixing bowl and mix well. Season, divide into 8 and shape into patties.

Heat the oil in a large frying pan, add the patties and fry over moderate heat for about 5 minutes, turning occasionally, until well browned. Transfer to a flameproof casserole.

In a bowl, mix the stock, sugar, ginger, raisins and lemon juice together, then pour over the patties. Cover and cook in the oven for 45 minutes or until the patties are tender.

Melt the margarine in the frying pan, add the pineapple rings and fry over a moderate heat for 2-3 minutes, turning once, until lightly browned on each side. Transfer to a heated serving dish.

Lift the patties from the casserole and place one on each pineapple slice.

Dissolve the arrowroot in the water and stir into the sauce. Bring to the boil, stirring. Adjust the seasoning to taste, then pour the sauce over the patties. Garnish with lemon twists and sliced ginger and serve.

Serving ideas: Serve with fried rice and a green vegetable.
Variation: Use minced pork instead of the beef; garnish with apple slices.

Chilli con carne

SERVES 4

2 tbls vegetable oil
1 large onion, sliced
1 garlic clove, crushed
750 g (1½ lb) minced beef
1 tsp hot chilli powder
397 g (14 oz) can tomatoes
150 ml (¼ pint) beef stock
1 tsp caster sugar
2 tbls tomato purée
salt and pepper
439 g (15½ oz) can red kidney beans, drained

Heat the oil in a flameproof casserole. Add the onion and garlic and fry gently for 7 minutes until golden. Add the mince and chilli powder and fry until the mince is well browned, stirring constantly with a wooden spoon.

Stir in the tomatoes with their juice, the stock, sugar, tomato purée and salt and pepper to taste. Bring to the boil, then lower the heat, cover and simmer gently for 30 minutes.

Add the drained kidney beans 5 minutes before the end of cooking time. Adjust the seasoning to taste and serve immediately.

Serving ideas: Serve with plain boiled rice and cucumber and yoghurt salad.
Variation: This is a spicy dish, but reduce the quantity of chilli powder to taste if a milder flavour is preferred. Add chopped red or green pepper with the tomatoes for extra flavour.

• Top left: Gingered beef patties; Bottom: Chilli con carne

Lasagne

SERVES 4

225 g (8 oz) lasagne sheets
25 g (1 oz) grated Parmesan cheese
For the meat sauce
1 tbls vegetable oil
1 onion, chopped
1 garlic clove, crushed
1 celery stalk, chopped
50 g (2 oz) streaky bacon rashers, rinded and chopped
350 g (12 oz) minced beef
25 g (1 oz) plain flour
300 ml (1/2 pint) beef stock
2 tbls tomato purée
2 tsp chopped fresh oregano or 1 tsp dried oregano
salt and pepper
For the béchamel sauce
450 ml (3/4 pint) milk
1 onion, quartered
2 parsley sprigs
1 bay leaf
25 g (1 oz) butter
25 g (1 oz) plain flour
1/4 tsp freshly grated nutmeg
salt and pepper

To make the meat sauce, heat the oil in a large saucepan, add the onion, garlic, celery and bacon and fry gently for 5 minutes until soft. Add the mince and fry for a further 5 minutes, stirring, until the meat is browned.

Stir in the flour, then add the stock, tomato purée, oregano and seasoning. Bring to the boil, stirring, then reduce the heat, cover and simmer gently for 30 minutes, stirring occasionally.

Meanwhile, make the béchamel sauce. Pour the milk into a saucepan and add the onion, parsley and bay leaf. Bring to the boil, then remove from the heat and leave to infuse for 10 minutes.

Melt the butter in a saucepan and stir in the flour. Cook over a low heat for 1-2 minutes, then strain the flavoured milk into the saucepan.

Bring to the boil, stirring until the sauce is smooth and thick. Simmer for 2 minutes then add the nutmeg and season to taste with salt and pepper.

Heat the oven to 190°C, 375°F, Gas Mark 5. Cook the lasagne sheets in a large saucepan of boiling salted water to which a few drops of oil have been added and cook for 5-15 minutes until tender (fresh pasta will cook more quickly than dried). Drain the lasagne and spread out to dry on a tea towel.

Arrange layers of meat sauce, lasagne and béchamel sauce in an ovenproof dish, finishing with a layer of béchamel sauce. Sprinkle the top with the Parmesan cheese.

Bake in the oven for 30 minutes until the topping is bubbling and golden brown. Serve at once.

Serving ideas: Serve with a green salad and extra Parmesan cheese.

• **Lasagne; Danish Frikadeller**

Danish Frikadeller

SERVES 4

450g (1 lb) pork mince
2 tbls plain flour
1 small onion, finely grated
½ tsp grated nutmeg or ground allspice
salt and pepper
150 ml (¼ pint) milk
25 g (1 oz) margarine or butter
4 tbls vegetable oil
To garnish
lettuce
parsley sprigs
tomato quarters

Place the mince in a bowl, and stir in the flour, onion, nutmeg, salt and plenty of freshly ground black pepper. Gradually add the milk, stirring well to mix. Cover the bowl and leave in a cool place for at least 1 hour.

Heat the margarine and oil in a large heavy-based frying pan. Using a greased tablespoon, take 8 heaped tablespoons of mince mixture, shape into rounded ovals and add to the pan.

Fry over a low heat for about 15 minutes, turning once, until golden and crisp on the outside.

Remove with a slotted spoon and arrange the patties on a bed of lettuce on a serving dish. Garnish with parsley sprigs and tomato quarters.

Serving ideas: Serve with potatoes sautéed in a mixture of oil and butter with a pinch of caraway seeds, and spinach cooked with pinenuts and currants. Or for a more filling meal serve with red cabbage and creamy mashed potatoes.
Variation: Use a mixture of minced pork and veal instead of all pork.

Meatballs in horseradish

SERVES 4

1 large slice white bread, 1 cm (½ inch) thick, crusts removed
450 g (1 lb) fine lean minced beef
¼ tsp mustard powder
salt and pepper
1 egg, beaten
25 g (1 oz) margarine or butter
For the sauce
15 g (½ oz) margarine or butter
2 tsp plain flour
300 ml (½ pint) chicken stock
2 tbls horseradish sauce
½ tsp lemon juice
1 tbls chopped parsley, to garnish

Soak the bread for a few minutes in water then drain well. Place the bread and mince in a mixing bowl and beat vigorously with a wooden spoon, to form a paste. Add the mustard powder, salt and plenty of pepper and stir in the egg to bind.

With floured hands, shape the meat mixture into about 16 balls. Melt the margarine in a large frying pan, add the meatballs and fry over a moderate heat, turning frequently, for 6-8 minutes, or until evenly browned and crisp. Remove from the pan.

To make the sauce, melt the margarine in the frying pan and stir in the flour. Cook gently for 1-2 minutes, then gradually stir in the stock. Bring to the boil, then stir in the horseradish sauce and lemon juice and season to taste.

Return the meatballs to the pan, cover and simmer over a low heat for 3 minutes to heat through.

Transfer to a heated serving dish and sprinkle over the chopped parsley and serve at once.

Serving ideas: Serve with buttered noodles and a green vegetable such as shredded, stir-fried cabbage or steamed and buttered courgettes.

Minced beef cobbler

SERVES 4-6

1 small onion, chopped
450g (1 lb) minced beef
397g (14 oz) can tomatoes
salt and pepper
283g (10 oz) can sliced carrots
For the scone topping
200g (8 oz) self raising flour
pinch of salt
50g (2 oz) margarine or butter
25g (1 oz) Cheddar cheese, grated
pinch of mustard
125 ml (¼ pint) milk
milk, to glaze

Brown the onion and minced beef together in a saucepan set over a low heat. Add the tomatoes, stir well to mix and bring to the boil. Season to taste and simmer, covered, for 30 minutes.

Meanwhile prepare the scone topping. Sift the flour with the salt into a bowl and rub in the margarine until the mixture resembles fine breadcrumbs. Stir in the cheese and mustard, and then add the milk and mix to a soft but not sticky dough. Roll out the dough to 1 cm (½ inch) thick on a floured surface and cut into approximately 5 cm (2 inch) rounds.

Heat the oven to 200°C, 400°F, Gas Mark 6. Drain the carrots and stir into the mince. Pour the mince into a casserole dish and arrange the scones around the edge. Brush the tops of the scones with a little milk.

Cook in the oven for 20-30 minutes until the scones are risen and golden.

Variation: For a different topping, omit the cheese and mustard and add 1 tsp mixed herbs.

• **Left: Minced beef cobbler**
Right: Meatballs in horseradish

Spaghetti Bolognese

SERVES 4

225g (8oz) spaghetti
25g (1oz) butter
50g (2oz) grated Parmesan cheese
For the Bolognese sauce
25g (1oz) margarine or butter
50g (2oz) Parma ham, chopped
1 onion, finely chopped
2 celery stalks, finely chopped
1 large carrot, finely chopped
225g (8oz) minced beef
175g (6oz) chicken livers, trimmed and chopped
1 tbls tomato purée
150ml (¼ pint) dry white wine
150ml (¼ pint) chicken stock
1 garlic clove, crushed
pinch of ground cinnamon
salt and pepper

To make the Bolognese sauce, melt the margarine in a large saucepan. Add the chopped ham and fry gently for 3 minutes. Add the onion, celery and carrot and fry for a further 7 minutes until browned. Add the mince and fry, turning frequently, for 2 minutes.

Add the chicken livers, tomato purée, wine, stock, garlic, cinnamon and seasoning. Stir well to mix. Bring to the boil, reduce the heat, cover and simmer gently for 30 minutes until the sauce is thick.

Meanwhile, cook the spaghetti in a large saucepan of boiling salted water for 15-20 minutes, until it is just tender. Drain well.

Melt the butter in the saucepan, return the spaghetti to the pan and stir over a very low heat until well coated. Turn into a warmed serving dish or casserole. Pour the Bolognese sauce over the spaghetti and sprinkle with the Parmesan cheese.

Serving ideas: Serve with a green salad and a hearty red wine.

Savoury plait

SERVES 4-6

1 tbls vegetable oil
1 small onion, finely chopped
225g (8oz) minced beef
225g (8oz) pork and beef sausagemeat
3 tsp dried mixed herbs
salt and pepper
1 egg
2 tsp soy sauce
397g (13oz) packet frozen puff pastry, defrosted
beaten egg, to glaze
watercress sprigs, to garnish
To garnish
watercress sprigs
tomato quarters

Heat the oven to 200°C, 400°F, Gas Mark 6. Heat the oil in a small frying pan, add the onion and fry gently for 5 minutes until softened.

Place the mince, sausagemeat and herbs in a large bowl and stir well. Mix in the onion and season lightly. Beat the egg with soy sauce and add to the mixture to bind.

On a floured surface, roll out the pastry to a rectangle 25 × 40cm (10 × 15 inch). Place on a baking sheet. Mark into 3 sections lengthways, and spoon the meat mixture down the centre, to within 2.5cm (1 inch) of the short edges. Cut the pastry down each side of the meat into diagonal strips 1cm (½ inch) apart; brush with beaten egg.

Take one strip from each side of the pastry and cross them over the meat. Continue folding over the pastry strips from alternate sides of the meat to give a plaited effect. Dampen top and bottom ends of the plait and fold over to seal.

Brush all over with beaten egg and bake in the oven for about 40-45 minutes, until crisp and golden.

Serve garnished with watercress sprigs and tomato quarters.

- Spaghetti Bolognese; Savoury plait

• Meat loaf

Meat loaf

SERVES 4-6

450g (1 lb) lean minced beef
100g (4 oz) sausagemeat
100g (4 oz) fresh white breadcrumbs
1 onion, finely chopped
½ tbls Worcestershire sauce
1 tbls tomato ketchup
½ tsp dried mixed herbs
2 tsp finely chopped fresh parsley
1 tsp English mustard
salt and pepper
2 eggs, beaten
To garnish
tomato slices
cucumber slices

Heat the oven to 190°C, 375°F, Gas Mark 5. Place all the ingredients except the eggs in a bowl and mix together. Bind the mixture with the beaten eggs.

Pack the mixture into a 1 kg (2 lb) loaf tin and cover with foil. Bake in the oven for 1 hour or until cooked through.

Loosen the sides of the loaf with a knife, then turn out on to a warm serving dish. Garnish the top of the loaf with tomato slices and serve.

Serving ideas: Serve with new potatoes and a green salad.
Variation: Spoon half the meat mixture into the tin then spread 100 g (4 oz) curd cheese over the top. Cover with the remaining meat mixture.

Kidneys in sherry sauce

SERVES 4

50 g (2 oz) margarine or butter
1 onion, chopped
8-12 lambs' kidneys, skinned and cored
50 g (2 oz) button mushrooms
1 tbls plain flour
300 ml (½ pint) beef stock
6 tbls sherry
1 tbls redcurrant jelly
salt and pepper
1 tbls fresh parsley, to garnish

Melt the margarine in a large frying pan, add the onion and fry gently for 7 minutes until golden.

Cut each kidney into 3 pieces. Add to the pan with the mushrooms and fry for 5 minutes, stirring. Stir in the flour, then add the stock, sherry and redcurrant jelly. Stir and season to taste.

Bring to the boil, then lower the heat and simmer gently for 5 minutes. Transfer to a heated serving dish and sprinkle with the chopped fresh parsley. Serve immediately.

Variation: Replace the sherry with orange juice and garnish with orange slices fried in butter and brown sugar.

• Kidneys in sherry sauce

Veal escalopes with vermouth and orange

SERVES 4

4 veal escalopes, each weighing 100g (4oz)
2 tbls plain flour, seasoned
50g (2oz) butter
2 tbls olive oil
150ml (1/4 pint) orange juice
150ml (1/4 pint) dry white vermouth
2 tsp soft dark brown sugar
salt and pepper
1-2 oranges, peeled and thinly sliced, to garnish

Beat the escalopes thinly with a mallet or rolling pin. Pat dry with absorbent paper. Coat the escalopes with the seasoned flour.

Melt half the butter with the oil in a large heavy-based frying pan. Add the escalopes and fry over moderate heat for 5-6 minutes, turning once, until lightly browned.

Pour the orange juice over the escalopes and simmer gently for about 8 minutes, or until the veal is tender. Remove the veal from the pan with a slotted spoon, arrange on a heated serving dish and keep warm.

Pour the vermouth into the pan, stir in the sugar and increase the heat. Boil vigorously, stirring constantly until the sauce has reduced and thickened.

Remove the pan from the heat, stir in the remaining butter cut into pieces, then whisk until the butter has melted and the sauce is glossy. Adjust the seasoning to taste, then pour the sauce over the veal. Garnish with orange slices and serve immediately.

Serving ideas: Serve with croquette potatoes in which finely chopped toasted hazelnuts and chives have been mixed and lightly steamed, buttered French beans.

• Steak Diane; Steak with anchovies; Veal escalopes with vermouth and orange

Steak Diane

SERVES 4

4 sirloin steaks, each weighing 100g (4oz)
50g (2oz) butter
1 tbls vegetable oil
4 tbls sherry
2 tbls brandy
salt and pepper
1 tbls chopped fresh chives
1 tbls chopped fresh parsley

Beat the steaks with a mallet or rolling pin until very thin. Heat half the butter with the oil in a frying pan. Add the steaks and fry over high heat for 1 minute on each side, to seal and brown.

Remove from the heat and add the sherry and brandy. Set alight and when the flames subside, transfer the steaks to a heated serving dish and season.

Bring the sauce to the boil. Boil for 1-2 minutes until slightly reduced, then stir in the remaining butter, cut into small pieces, with the herbs. Pour the sauce over the steaks and serve.

Serving ideas: Serve with French fries and a green salad.

Steak with anchovies

SERVES 4

40g (1½oz) butter, softened
1 tbls chopped fresh parsley
½tsp lemon juice
pepper
750g (1½lb) rump steak, cut into 4 equal pieces
1 tbls vegetable oil
50g (1¾oz) can anchovy fillets, drained

Cream 25g (1 oz) of the butter with the parsley and lemon juice, and season with pepper. Shape into a roll, wrap in cling film and chill in the freezing compartment of the refrigerator until firm. Cut into 4 slices.

Score the fat on the steak to prevent it curling and season with pepper. Heat the remaining butter with the oil in a frying pan until hot. Add the steaks and fry for 4 minutes over high heat, turning once, to seal and brown.

Reduce the heat to moderate and cook for a further 1-3 minutes on each side, until cooked to your liking.

To serve, arrange the anchovy fillets on the steaks and top each one with a pat of parsley butter.

Serving ideas: Serve with fried potatoes and creamed spinach.
Variation: Add 1 clove crushed garlic to the parsley butter.

Pork fillet with peanut sauce

SERVES 4

500g (1 1/4 lb) pork fillet, cut into small round slices
25g (1 oz) plain flour, seasoned
50g (2 oz) margarine or butter
1 onion, finely chopped
3 tbls smooth peanut butter
450 ml (3/4 pint) hot chicken stock
50g (2 oz) salted peanuts, to garnish

Coat the pork slices in the seasoned flour. Melt the margarine in a large frying pan, add the onion and fry gently for 6 minutes until just beginning to colour. Add the pork slices and cook for about 5 minutes, turning occasionally, until evenly brown.

Blend the peanut butter with the stock, stir into the pan and season to taste. Cover and simmer for about 20 minutes, or until the pork is tender.

Transfer to a heated serving dish, sprinkle with the peanuts and serve immediately.

Serving ideas: Serve with buttered noodles and a green salad.

Pork chops with barbecue sauce

SERVES 4

4 large pork chops, trimmed
salt and pepper
orange or lemon slices, to garnish
For the barbecue sauce
1 large onion, finely chopped
1 garlic clove, crushed
3 tbls tarragon vinegar
3 tsp Worcestershire sauce
50g (2 oz) soft light brown sugar
grated rind and juice of 1 lemon
1/2 tsp chilli powder
2 tsp salt
150 ml (1/4 pint) water

Put all the ingredients for the sauce except the water and salt into a saucepan and stir well. Add the salt and the water and bring to the boil, stirring. Simmer gently, uncovered, for 15 minutes, stirring occasionally, or until the onion is soft and the sauce slightly thickened.

Meanwhile, heat the grill to moderate. Season the chops and lay on the grill rack. Grill for 8-10 minutes on each side or until cooked through and well browned all over.

Arrange the pork chops on a heated serving dish, spoon over the sauce and garnish with the orange or lemon slices. Serve immediately.

Crispy liver

SERVES 4

75g (3 oz) margarine or butter
1 large onion, sliced into rings
25g (1 oz) plain flour
salt and pepper
1/2 tsp dried mixed herbs
1 egg
1 tbls milk
450g (1 lb) lambs' liver, thinly sliced
50g (2 oz) rolled porridge oats
120 ml (4 fl oz) sherry
120 ml (4 fl oz) chicken stock
parsley sprigs, to garnish

Melt 25g (1 oz) of the margarine in a large frying pan, add the onion and fry gently for 5 minutes, turning occasionally, until softened. Remove from the pan and keep warm.

Mix the flour in a shallow bowl with the salt, pepper and herbs. In a separate shallow bowl, beat together the egg and milk.

Pat the liver slices dry with absorbent paper. Coat them first in the seasoned flour, then in the egg and milk and finally in the oats, pressing them on with the fingers. Reserve any excess seasoned flour.

Melt the remaining margarine in the pan and fry the liver slices for about 6 minutes, turning once, until crisp and brown but still pink inside.

Remove the liver from the pan and

• **Pork fillet with peanut sauce; Crispy liver; Pork chops with barbecue sauce**

keep warm. Sprinkle in the reserved seasoned flour and stir. Pour in the sherry and stock, bring to the boil, stirring, and season to taste.

Arrange the liver on a heated serving dish and scatter the onion rings on top. Pour over the sauce and garnish with parsley sprigs. Serve immediately.

Serving ideas: Serve with fried onion rings and grilled tomatoes.
Variation: Omit the sherry and stir 150 ml (1/4 pint) soured cream into the sauce; do not allow to boil again.

Lamb kebabs

SERVES 4

1.25 kg (2½ lb) leg or shoulder of lamb, boned and cut into 4 cm (1½ inch) cubes
1 green pepper, cored, seeded and cut into 2.5 cm (1 inch) squares
1 small onion, quartered
3 tomatoes, quartered
For the marinade
2 tsp sunflower or olive oil
3 tbls natural yoghurt
100 ml (3½ fl oz) lemon juice
2 garlic cloves, crushed
1 tablespoon chopped fresh mint, or 1 tsp dried mint
1 fresh rosemary sprig or ½ tsp dried rosemary
1 tsp paprika
¼ tsp mustard powder
salt and pepper

Combine all the marinade ingredients in a large shallow bowl. Stir well, then add the cubed lamb. Cover and leave to marinate overnight or for at least 6 hours.

Heat the grill to high. Drain the lamb cubes, reserving the marinade. Thread the lamb cubes on to 4 large greased kebab skewers, alternating with the green pepper, onion and tomatoes.

Cook under the grill for about 12 minutes, turning and brushing with the reserved marinade, until the lamb is tender. Lay the kebabs on a heated serving dish and serve immediately.

Serving ideas: Serve with fried rice in which chopped spring onion and diced red pepper are mixed, and a salad of lettuce, watercress and sliced oranges.
Variation: For pork kebabs, use 1 kg (2 lb) pork fillet and 1 tsp ground coriander in the marinade instead of the herbs.

• **Lamb kebabs; Herb-crunch lamb cutlets; Stir-fried liver**

Herb-crunch lamb cutlets

SERVES 4

1 egg
75 g (3 oz) dry breadcrumbs
1 tsp dried mint
1 tsp dried thyme
2 tsp grated Parmesan cheese
salt and pepper
4 best end lamb cutlets, trimmed
mint sprigs, to garnish

Heat the oven to 200°C, 400°F, Gas Mark 6.

Beat the egg in a shallow bowl. In a separate shallow bowl, mix together the breadcrumbs, mint, thyme, cheese, salt and pepper.

Dip the cutlets first into the beaten egg, then into the breadcrumb mixture to coat evenly, pressing the mixture on with the fingers.

Lay the cutlets on a greased baking sheet and bake in the oven for 30 minutes or until tender.

Arrange on a heated serving platter, garnish with mint sprigs and serve immediately.

Serving ideas: Serve with new potatoes and courgettes.
Variation: These cutlets can also be served cold as part of a buffet lunch.

Stir-fried liver

SERVES 4

450 g (1 lb) pig's liver
2 tbls cornflour
2 tbls light soy sauce
6 tbls vegetable oil
4 onions, thinly sliced
2 tsp salt
2 tbls sherry
2 tsp caster sugar
about 85 ml (3 fl oz) chicken stock or water
2 tsp sesame seed oil
2 tbls chopped spring onion tops, to garnish

Cut the liver into 3.5 × 2.5 cm (1½ × 1 inch) slices about 1 cm (½ inch) thick. Mix the cornflour with the soy sauce in a bowl, to make a smooth paste. Coat the liver slices with the mixture.

Heat half the oil in a wok or frying pan, add the liver and fry over a high heat for 20-30 seconds, turning. Remove with a slotted spoon.

Heat the remaining oil in the wok, add the onions and allow to soften. Return the liver to the wok with the salt, sherry and sugar. Add the stock and stir well to mix. Add the sesame seed oil.

Transfer to a heated dish, sprinkle with the spring onions and serve.

Turkey à la king

SERVES 6-8

50g (2oz) margarine or butter
1 small onion, finely chopped
1 small green pepper, cored, seeded and diced
225g (8oz) button mushrooms
3 tbls cornflour
300ml (½ pint) milk
300ml (½ pint) chicken stock
450g (1 lb) cooked turkey, cubed
pinch of dried thyme
1 tbls dry sherry
salt
freshly ground black pepper
To garnish
25g (1 oz) blanched almonds, toasted
1 tbls chopped fresh parsley

Melt the margarine in a large saucepan, add the onion and green pepper and fry gently for 5 minutes until softened. Add the mushrooms and fry for a further 3 minutes until soft.

Mix the cornflour with a little water and add to the pan, stirring constantly. Add the milk and stock and bring to the boil, stirring.

Add the turkey, thyme and sherry. Simmer for 5 minutes; season to taste.

Transfer to a heated serving dish, sprinkle with the toasted almonds and parsley and serve immediately.

Serving ideas: Serve with creamed potatoes or rice and a green vegetable.
Variation: Add 50g (2oz) grated Gruyère cheese to the milk and stock; add the turkey to the melted cheese.

• **Turkey à la king; Cheesy baked chicken**

Cheesy baked chicken

SERVES 4

4 boned chicken breasts
4 tbls vegetable oil
1 tbls lemon juice
1 tsp dried thyme
salt and pepper
4 thin slices cooked ham, trimmed to the same size as the chicken pieces
50 g (2 oz) Gruyère cheese, thinly sliced
2 large tomatoes, sliced

Heat the oven to 190°C, 375°F, Gas Mark 5. Cut 4 pieces of aluminium foil, each about 30 cm (12 inches) square. Skin the chicken breasts and cut 3 slits in each. Lay a chicken breast on each foil square.

Combine the oil, lemon juice, thyme and salt and pepper. Raise the edges of the foil around the chicken and pour on the sauce, dividing it between the 4 breasts. Seal the foil edges firmly to make parcels.

Bake in the oven for 25-30 minutes, or until cooked through. Test for doneness by opening up the foil and piercing the chicken with a skewer; when the juices run clear the chicken is cooked.

Heat the grill to moderate. Open the parcels and place a ham slice, then a portion of cheese on top of each chicken breast. Top with the tomato slices and spoon over a little sauce.

Grill for 4-5 minutes until the cheese is bubbling. Serve immediately, straight from the foil.

Serving idea: Serve with sauté potatoes and whole sweetcorn kernels cooked with diced red peppers.

Variation: Replace the tomatoes with 8 asparagus spears.

Beef Stroganoff

SERVES 4

15 g (½ oz) butter
1 onion, sliced
225 g (8 oz) button mushrooms, sliced
750 g (1½ lb) fillet steak, cut into thin strips
salt and pepper
1 tsp Dijon mustard
2 tbls brandy
150 ml (¼ pint) soured cream
1 tbls chopped fresh parsley, to garnish

Melt the butter in a large frying pan. Add the onion and fry gently for 7 minutes or until golden. Add the mushrooms and fry for a further 3 minutes until softened.

Add the steak to the pan, season well and stir in the mustard. Fry, turning often, for 5 minutes.

Stir in the brandy and soured cream and heat through gently; do not allow to boil. Transfer to a heated serving dish; serve garnished with parsley.

Variation: For a cheaper version use 750 g (1½ lb) lean chuck steak. After frying the meat add about 150 ml (¼ pint) beef stock and 150 ml (¼ pint) white wine. Cover and simmer very gently for 1½ hours until the meat is tender. Then complete as above.

Beef Wellington

SERVES 4-6

1 kg (2 lb) fillet of beef, trimmed
40 g (1½ oz) butter, softened
1 onion, finely chopped
225 g (8 oz) mushrooms, chopped
salt and pepper
397 (13 oz) packet frozen puff pastry, defrosted,
beaten egg, to glaze
watercress sprigs, to garnish

Heat the oven to 190°C, 375°F, Gas Mark 5. Pat the beef dry with absorbent paper and spread with 15 g (½ oz) of the butter. Place in a roasting tin and roast for 40 minutes, basting occasionally. Remove and leave until cold.

Melt the remaining butter in a saucepan. Add the onion and cook gently for 5 minutes until softened. Add the mushrooms and cook for about 15 minutes until some of the liquid has evaporated. Remove from the heat, season and leave until cold.

Increase oven temperature to 230°C, 450°F, Gas Mark 8. Roll out the pastry to a rectangle large enough to enclose the beef. Place on a baking sheet.

Spread half the mushroom mixture down the centre of the pastry. Place the beef on top, then top with the remaining mushroom mixture. Brush the edges of the pastry with egg and wrap the pastry round the meat, pressing the long edges together firmly and tucking in the short ends to seal. Use trimmings to make pastry leaves to decorate.

Brush all over with beaten egg, then cook in the oven for about 40 minutes, cover with foil for the last 10 minutes so the pastry stays golden brown. Transfer to a serving dish, garnish with watercress sprigs, slice and serve.

• Left: Beef Stroganoff
Right: Beef Wellington

• Beef bourguignonne; Beef olives

Boeuf bourguignonne

SERVES 4

15 g (½ oz) beef dripping or lard
750 g-1 kg (1½-2 lb) chuck steak, trimmed and cut into 2.5 cm (1 inch) cubes
100 g (4 oz) unsmoked streaky bacon, rinded and chopped
2 garlic cloves, crushed (optional)
1 tbls plain flour
salt and pepper
400 ml (14 fl oz) red wine
1 bouquet garni
25 g (1 oz) margarine or butter
225 g (8 oz) small pickling onions
225 g (8 oz) button mushrooms
1 tsp soft light brown sugar

Heat the oven to 160°C, 325°F, Gas Mark 3. Melt the dripping in a flameproof casserole. Add the beef and fry quickly over high heat, turning, for 3 minutes, to seal and brown on all sides. Remove with a slotted spoon and set aside to cool.

Add the bacon and garlic, if using, to the casserole and fry for 2-3 minutes. Stir in the flour, season to taste and return the beef to the casserole.

Heat 300 ml (½ pint) wine in a small saucepan. Set it alight and pour over the beef in the casserole. Add the bouquet garni, cover and cook in the oven for 2 hours. Stir in a little water if it shows signs of becoming dry.

Melt the margarine in a saucepan. Add the onions and mushrooms and fry gently for 2-3 minutes. Pour over the remaining wine, stir in the sugar and bring to the boil.

Stir into the casserole and cook for a further 30 minutes or until the beef and onions are tender. Discard the bouquet garni and adjust the seasoning before serving straight from the casserole.

Serving ideas: Serve with parsley potatoes and a green salad.

Beef olives

SERVES 4

4 thin slices beef silverside, each weighing about 100 g (4 oz), trimmed
25 g (1 oz) plain flour, seasoned
2-3 tbls vegetable oil
1 onion, chopped
450 ml (3/4 pint) beef stock
1 tbls tomato purée
2 tbls red wine
1 tbls chopped fresh parsley, to garnish

For the stuffing
50 g (2 oz) fresh breadcrumbs
25 g (1 oz) shredded suet
1 tsp chopped fresh parsley
1/4 tsp dried oregano
1/4 tsp dried thyme
salt and pepper
1 egg, beaten

Heat the oven to 180°C, 350°F, Gas Mark 4. In a bowl, mix together all the stuffing ingredients except the egg, then stir in sufficient egg to bind.

Spoon a portion of the mixture down the centre of each beef slice, then roll into neat parcels and tie in two or three places with fine string.

Toss the beef olives in the seasoned flour. Heat 2 tbls of the oil in a large frying pan, and fry the beef olives for 2-3 minutes over a moderate heat, turning, until brown all over. Remove from the pan with a fish slice and arrange in a fairly shallow casserole.

Add the onion to the frying pan, with a little extra oil if necessary, and fry gently for 5 minutes until softened. Add the remaining seasoned flour and cook for 1 minute, stirring constantly.

Remove from the heat and stir in the stock, tomato purée and wine. Return to the heat and bring to the boil, stirring constantly. Adjust the seasoning to taste, then pour over the beef olives.

Cover and cook in the oven for 1 1/2-2 hours or until the beef olives are tender. Sprinkle with the parsley and serve straight from the casserole.

Serving ideas: Serve with sautéed mushrooms and green peas.

Wiener schnitzel

SERVES 4

4 veal escalopes, each weighing about 100 g (4 oz)
100 ml (4 fl oz) lemon juice
salt and pepper
1 large egg, beaten
100 g (4 oz) dried breadcrumbs
15 g (½ oz) butter
To garnish
2 lemons, quartered
parsley sprigs

Place the escalopes in a large shallow dish, sprinkle with the lemon juice and seasoning and leave to marinate at room temperature for 1 hour.

Drain the escalopes and dip first in the egg, then in the breadcrumbs, to coat evenly. Refrigerate for 10 minutes.

Melt the butter in a large frying pan and when foaming add 2 of the escalopes. Fry over high heat for 2-3 minutes on each side until tender and golden brown.

Drain on absorbent paper, transfer to a heated serving dish and keep warm while frying the remaining escalopes in the same way. Garnish with lemon wedges and parsley sprigs and serve.

Beef and spinach curry

SERVES 4

15 g (½ oz) butter
1 tbls vegetable oil
2 onions, finely chopped
1 garlic clove, crushed
1 small piece fresh root ginger, finely chopped, or 1 tsp ground ginger
1 tsp ground turmeric
½ tsp chilli powder
1 tbls ground coriander
1 tsp ground mustard seeds
750 g-1 kg (1½-2 lb) chuck steak, trimmed and cut into cubes
226 g (8 oz) packet frozen spinach, defrosted and thoroughly drained
2 × 150 g (5.29 oz) cartons natural yoghurt

Heat the oven to 160°C, 325°F, Gas Mark 3. Heat the butter and oil in a flameproof casserole. Add the onions, garlic and spices and fry gently for 5 minutes until softened. Add the meat and fry, stirring, for 5 minutes, to seal and brown on all sides.

Heat the spinach gently in a non-stick saucepan, then stir into the casserole with one carton of the yoghurt.

Cover and cook in the oven for 2-2½ hours or until the beef is tender. If the curry shows signs of becoming too dry during cooking time, add a little water. Just before serving, stir in the remaining yoghurt.

Serving ideas: Serve with rice, mango chutney, parathas and sliced tomatoes mixed with chopped spring onion.

New England beef dinner

SERVES 6-8

1.5 kg (3 lb) salt brisket of beef
1 bouquet garni
1 tsp whole black peppercorns
1 onion, stuck with 4 cloves
8 carrots, halved lengthways
8 small potatoes, halved
1 small cabbage, quartered and cored
salt and pepper
1 tbls fresh parsley, to garnish

Put the brisket into a deep, flameproof casserole, cover with cold water and add the bouquet garni, peppercorns and onion. Bring very slowly to the boil. Skim if necessary, then cover and simmer very slowly for 3 hours.

Add the carrots and potatoes, cover again and simmer for a further 20 minutes. Stir in the cabbage, cover again and simmer a further 20-30 minutes or until the beef and vegetables are tender. Drain.

Transfer the beef to a board, carve it into thick slices and arrange on a heated serving dish. Surround with the carrots, potatoes and cabbage.

Strain the broth, adjust the seasoning and pour a little over the meat; hand the remainder separately in a sauce boat. Garnish with parsley; serve.

• New England beef dinner; Beef and spinach curry; Wiener schnitzel

Chop suey

SERVES 4

2 tbls light soy sauce
1 tbls dry sherry
2 tsp cornflour
225 g (8 oz) pork escalopes, cubed
5 tbls vegetable oil
2 spring onions, cut into 2.5 cm (1 inch) lengths
1 slice ginger root, finely chopped
100 g (4 oz) fresh beansprouts
1 small green pepper, cored, seeded and finely sliced
a few small cauliflower florets
2-3 tomatoes, chopped
1-2 carrots, thinly sliced
50 g (2 oz) green beans, chopped
2 tsp salt
1 tbls caster sugar
3 tbls chicken stock or water
chopped spring onion tops, to garnish

In a bowl, mix together the soy sauce, sherry and cornflour, to make a smooth paste. Coat the pork evenly in the paste.

Heat half the oil in a large frying pan and fry the pork over a high heat for about 2 minutes, stirring constantly. Then remove with a slotted spoon and set aside on a plate.

Heat the remaining oil and add the spring onions and ginger, followed by the remaining vegetables, salt and sugar. Stir for 1 minute, then return the pork to the pan. Stir well to mix and moisten with a little stock if necessary. Transfer to a heated serving dish, garnish with spring onion tops and serve immediately.

Serving ideas: Serve with boiled rice or, if you prefer, fried rice browned with a tablespoon of soy sauce; garnish with shrimps and chopped spring onions.

Variation: Use 225 g (8 oz) boned chicken breast instead of the pork.

• Bottom: Chop suey; Right: Sweet and sour pork

Sweet and sour pork

SERVES 4

175 g (6 oz) self-raising flour
1 tsp ground allspice
½ tsp ground ginger
1 egg, lightly beaten
about 150 ml (¼ pint) water
450 g (1 lb) lean pork, cubed
vegetable oil, for deep frying
For the sweet and sour sauce
1 tbls corn oil
1 small onion, chopped
1 small green pepper, cored, seeded and chopped
½ tsp ground ginger
2 tbls wine vinegar
1 tbls tomato purée
1 tbls light soy sauce
3 tbls clear honey
1 tbls dry sherry
1 tbls cornflour blended with 6 tbls cold water
1 canned pineapple ring, drained and chopped

Sift the flour with the allspice and ginger into a mixing bowl. Make a well in the centre and add the egg. Beat thoroughly, adding sufficient water to make a smooth light batter. Dip each piece of pork into the batter to coat.

Heat the oil in a wok or large deep frying pan. Add 4-5 pieces of pork and fry for 4-5 minutes, until crisp and golden. Drain on absorbent paper, then transfer to a heated serving dish and keep warm while frying the remaining pork in the same way.

To make the sauce, heat the oil in the wok. Add the onion, pepper and ginger and stir fry for 1 minute. Add the remaining ingredients, stirring well.

Bring to the boil and cook gently for 2 minutes until combined. Pour over the pork and serve.

Serving ideas: Serve with boiled rice and a salad of beansprouts garnished with thinly sliced stem ginger and red pepper. Use a spoonful or two of the ginger syrup in the salad dressing.

Tagine of lamb

SERVES 4

750 g (1½ lb) boneless lamb, trimmed and cut into 2.5 cm (1 inch) cubes
2 onions, finely chopped
2 tbls olive oil
½ tsp ground coriander
½ tsp ground ginger
1 tsp ground cinnamon
225 g (8 oz) dried pears, soaked in water overnight and drained
2 tbls clear honey
600 ml (1 pint) boiling chicken stock
salt
freshly ground black pepper
1 tbls cornflour
2 tbls cold water
2 tsp orange flower water
To garnish
fresh coriander leaves
toasted pine nuts

Heat the oven to 160°C, 325°F, Gas Mark 3. Put the lamb, onion, oil, spices, pears, honey and stock into a casserole. Season to taste.

Cover and cook in the oven for 2-2½ hours until the lamb is tender. Arrange the lamb and pears on a heated serving dish and keep hot.

Pour the sauce into a small saucepan and place over a low heat. Blend the cornflour with the water, to make a smooth paste, then stir into the sauce and bring to the boil, stirring. Adjust the seasoning to taste.

Pour the sauce over the lamb and sprinkle with the orange flower water. Garnish with coriander leaves and toasted pine nuts and serve immediately.

Serving idea: Serve with pilau rice.
Variation: Use dried apricots instead of dried pears.

• **Left: Tagine of lamb; Right: Lamb korma**

Lamb korma

SERVES 4

2 tsp cumin seeds
1 tbls coriander seeds
2 × 150 g (5.29 oz) cartons natural yoghurt
1 tsp ground turmeric
½ tsp freshly ground black pepper
450 g (1 lb) boneless lamb, trimmed and cut into 1 cm (½ inch) cubes
40 g (1½ oz) ghee or unsalted butter
1 onion, chopped
2 garlic cloves, crushed
2.5 cm (1 inch) piece of fresh root ginger, peeled and finely chopped
½ tsp ground cloves
1 tsp ground cardamom
3 tbls ground almonds
142 ml (5 fl oz) carton double cream
½ tsp salt
2-3 tsp lemon juice
To garnish
1 tbls flaked almonds
1 lemon, quartered

Put the cumin and coriander seeds in a small saucepan and heat gently for 1 minute to release the aromatic oils. Transfer to a mortar or food processor and pulverize.

Put the yoghurt in a deep bowl and stir in the cumin and coriander with the turmeric and pepper. Mix in the lamb, cover and refrigerate for 2 hours.

Melt the ghee in a large heavy-based saucepan, add the onion and fry gently for 5 minutes until softened. Add the garlic, ginger, cloves and cardamom and fry for a further 3-4 minutes.

Add the lamb with the marinade and ground almonds. Bring to the boil and boil briskly for a few minutes, then cover tightly and simmer very gently for 1¼ hours or until the lamb is tender. Stir occasionally; add water if necessary.

Stir in the cream, add salt and lemon juice to taste and simmer for 2-3 minutes until heated through.

Transfer to a heated serving dish, scatter with the almonds, garnish with lemon wedges and serve.

Coq au vin

SERVES 4

25g (1 oz) butter
1 tbls vegetable oil
12 small pickling onions, peeled
1 garlic clove, crushed
100g (4 oz) unsmoked streaky bacon, rinded and diced
4 chicken joints, skinned
2 tbls brandy
300 ml (½ pint) red wine
150 ml (¼ pint) chicken stock
1 bouquet garni
salt and pepper
225g (8 oz) button mushrooms, sliced
1 tbls chopped fresh parsley, to garnish
For the beurre manié
25g (1 oz) butter, softened
25g (1 oz) plain flour

Heat the oven to 180°C, 350°F, Gas Mark 4. Heat half the butter and the oil in a large flameproof casserole. Add the onions, garlic and bacon. Fry for 8 minutes until golden brown, then remove and set aside.

Add the chicken joints to the casserole and fry gently for 5 minutes, turning, until golden on all sides. Pour over the brandy and set alight.

When the flames subside, return the onions, garlic and bacon to the casserole. Pour in the wine and half the stock and add the bouquet garni and salt and pepper. Cover and cook in the oven for 1-1½ hours or until the chicken is tender. Add more stock to the casserole during cooking, if needed.

Return the casserole to the top of the stove and discard the bouquet garni. To make the beurre manié, combine the butter and flour to make a thick paste. Cut into pieces, then add gradually to the casserole over a low heat, whisking between each addition. Simmer until the sauce thickens, stirring.

Melt the remaining butter in a small frying pan and add the mushrooms. Fry for 1 minute over a high heat, then add to the casserole. Sprinkle over the chopped parsley; serve immediately.

Tandoori chicken

SERVES 4

1.5 kg (3 lb) chicken
50 ml (2 fl oz) lemon juice
1 tsp salt
8 green cardamom pods
2 tsp cumin seeds
1 tsp fennel seeds
2.5 cm (1 inch) piece ginger root, peeled and chopped, or 2 tsp ground ginger
2-3 garlic cloves, crushed
1 tsp hot chilli powder
150g (5.29 oz) carton natural yoghurt
25g (1 oz) butter
coriander leaves, to garnish

Pat the chicken dry with absorbent paper, remove the wing tips and cut in half lengthways through the backbone. Place the chicken halves skin side up in a large shallow ovenproof dish. Make several incisions into the chicken flesh and rub in the lemon juice and salt.

Split open the cardamom pods and remove the seeds. Place the cardamom, cumin and fennel seeds in a heavy-based frying pan. Cook without fat over a moderate heat for 1-2 minutes to release the aromatic oils. Transfer to a mortar or food processor and pulverize.

Add ginger, garlic and chilli powder to the pulverized spices to make a smooth paste. Mix with the yoghurt and pour over the chicken. Leave to marinate for 5-6 hours or overnight in the refrigerator.

Heat the oven to 220°C, 425°F, Gas Mark 7. Dot the chicken with the butter and cook in the oven for 1 hour or until tender, basting twice in the first 30 minutes.

Halve each chicken portion crossways, to make quarters, garnish with coriander leaves and serve with warm nan or pitta bread and a tomato and onion salad.

• Top: Tandoori chicken; Chicken Kiev; Bottom: Coq au vin

Chicken Kiev

SERVES 4

100g (4 oz) butter, softened
finely grated rind and juice of ½ lemon
1 tbls chopped fresh parsley
1 tbls chopped chives
1 garlic clove, crushed (optional)
salt and pepper
4 large chicken breasts, boned and skinned
25g (1 oz) plain flour, seasoned
1 egg, beaten
100g (4 oz) dried breadcrumbs
vegetable oil, for deep frying
lemon twists, to garnish

Place the butter in a mixing bowl and beat in the lemon rind and juice, herbs, garlic, if using, and seasoning to taste. Beat vigorously until well blended, then shape into a rectangle and wrap in greaseproof paper or foil. Chill until firm in the freezing compartment of the refrigerator.

Lay the chicken breasts flat on a board, with the thickest part towards you. Using a small sharp knife, make a pocket in each breast by slitting it horizontally to within 2.5cm (1 inch) of each end, taking care not to pierce either end or the far side. Insert a finger of butter into each pocket and press the edges together firmly to enclose the butter completely.

Dip the rolled chicken breasts first in the seasoned flour, then in the egg, then in the breadcrumbs, making sure that the chicken is thoroughly coated. Chill in the refrigerator for 1 hour before frying.

Heat the oil in a deep-fat fryer to 190°C (375°F) or until a stale bread cube browns in 30 seconds. Add 2 of the chicken breasts and fry for 8-10 minutes or until crisp and golden brown. Drain on absorbent paper and keep warm on a heated serving dish while frying the remaining chicken breasts in the same way. Garnish with the lemon twists and serve.

Serving ideas: Serve with fried potatoes and a green salad.

INDEX

***Note:* this index includes variations supplied in recipes as well as the main recipes.**